AIR COMMAND AND STAFF COLLEGE
AIR UNIVERSITY

Ethnic Conflict and US Central Command Policy for the Central Asian Republics

WILLIAM M. TART
Major, USAF

Air Command and Staff College
Wright Flyer Paper No. 16

MAXWELL AIR FORCE BASE, ALABAMA

October 2001

This Wright Flyer Paper and others in the series are available electronically at the Air University Research Web site http://research.maxwell.af.mil under "Research Papers" then "Special Collections."

Disclaimer

Foreword

It is my great pleasure to present another of the *Wright Flyer Papers* series. In this series, Air Command and Staff College (ACSC) recognizes and publishes the "best of the best" student research projects from the prior academic year. The ACSC research program encourages our students to move beyond the school's core curriculum in their own professional development and in "advancing aerospace power." The series title reflects our desire to perpetuate the pioneering spirit embodied in earlier generations of airmen. Projects selected for publication combine solid research, innovative thought, and lucid presentation in exploring war at the operational level. With this broad perspective, the *Wright Flyer Papers* engage an eclectic range of doctrinal, technological, organizational, and operational questions. Some of these studies provide new solutions to familiar problems. Others encourage us to leave the familiar behind in pursuing new possibilities. By making these research studies available in the *Wright Flyer Papers*, ACSC hopes to encourage critical examination of the findings and to stimulate further research in these areas.

John T. Sheridan, Brig Gen (Sel), USAF
Commandant

Preface

I could have selected many topics as a research project; but I chose one that stretched my academic skills, research abilities, and comprehension of a topic about which I knew little. Ignorant of the region, I began this project hoping to start something that would broaden my horizons and possibly even help build or explain US military policy. The first aspect is an understatement—the second may yet be in the future.

In either case, I did not make this journey without many pillars of support. My total page count would be extremely unbalanced if I named everyone who contributed to this work. The majority of my thanks go to a handful of great supporters. First, without my wife, Andi, who focused me, showed me reality, and protected me from distractions when I needed to write, none of this could have happened. Second, thanks to Maj Jeff Hupy for giving me some unconventional advice on mind-mapping and whose continuous flow of information from Air Mobility Command not only gave me great data but also kept me writing. Third, Maj Vicki Rast deserves my utmost thanks for perfecting the unconventional techniques, for focusing me on the problem statements, and for providing an academic role model. Fourth, thanks to Raven buddy—Maj Steven Latchford from CENTCOM J-5—who was an indispensable asset and thought that 75 pages of CENTCOM data would be a quick read. Fifth, to Gen Theo Mataxis, US Army (USA), retired, and Lt Col Forrest Wentworth, USA, I extend my thanks for giving me the frameworks that will stick with me forever on small-scale conflicts (I hope I got it right) and the ability to pronounce "diaspora" correctly.

Abstract

This paper identifies a possible shortfall in United States (US) military planning, the experience of US Central Command (CENTCOM) planners in dealing with the Central Asian States. Their emphasis is understandably focused on Iraq, Iran, and Pakistan. This paper develops for these planners the most likely threat to stability in CENTCOM's area of responsibility—ethnic conflict caused by spillover from neighboring countries. This paper also attempts to counter critics in the January–February 2000 *Foreign Affairs* who maintained that our obtuse military ties are not sensible nor sustainable. They described our current activities as a manner reminiscent of ill-advised US activities in Latin America in the 1970s. All of these condemnations from authors Amy Myers Jaffe and Robert A. Manning, although mostly unfounded, are perceptions that senior economists and political scientists hold. This paper helps CENTCOM "fire for effect" in developing and implementing a dynamic engagement strategy in this important region.

This paper develops the theoretical framework of ethnic conflict, generated both internally and from spillover. This framework is then applied to Central Asia, illustrating it as a complex region of numerous ethnic groups in a bad neighborhood with some powerful bad neighbors. These neighbors, as well as the United States, have vital interests in engaging in this region. These interests—derived from the national security strategy—revolve around vital, important, and tertiary interests including humanitarian issues. The proliferation of weapons of mass destruction and transnational drug smuggling are major threats, while Central Asian resources and US influence and credibility are major goals of US and CENTCOM involvement here.

This involvement has been seemingly disjointed and even at odds with other governmental agencies. CENTCOM activities—currently limited to only three of the five republics—are rated on effect and analyzed into general courses of action. This paper sets the stage for all CENTCOM policies by establishing "bounding" questions that can be used to guide productive CENTCOM engagement through the complexities of Central Asia and its possible ethnic conflict.

Introduction

After the collapse of the former Soviet Union, there was a mountain of unresolved issues that made the promise of a brighter future not as close as everyone had believed. One of these problems is the United States (US) engagement activities in the Newly Independent States (NIS). The problem is that military planners have little experience with this issue, particularly in the Central Asian States (CAS) of Kazakhstan, Kyrgyzstan, Tajikistan, Turkmenistan, and Uzbekistan (see map). In this paper, I took a three-step approach to solving this problem. First, I familiarized the reader with ethnic conflict and its proximate and underlying causes. Second, I described what is at stake in Central Asia in terms of US interests. Third, I evaluated current US Central Command (CENTCOM) activities in the CAS and recommended some improvements.

Background and Methodology

I had to start with a detailed narrative of the theoretical background of ethnic conflict. Theories, supporting examples, and their applications in Central Asia bolstered my argument that ethnic conflict and spillover remain the major threats to US interests in the area. Economic and demographic statistics supported claims by theorists in my descriptions of bad neighborhoods and dangerous situations. Once the background was complete, I needed to emphasize that establishing a coherent plan for total US military engagement was important by researching the value of the region and the threats to our interest in the area. Defining "US interests," detailing the threat of weapons of mass destruction (WMD), and analyzing both the natural resources and transnational threats in Central Asia supported my goals. The few competing views found in my research were included in this part of the work on both the area's importance and effect of traditional policies on the region. Finally, CENTCOM planning documents and engagement tools allowed me to look at ongoing activities for a coherent and spelled-out strategy. As a collective I could rate the events as very effective, effective, or somewhat effective, when given the current context. Overall, the re-

1

search led me to conclude that CENTCOM must create a more effective strategy of engagement in Central Asia to protect vital, important, and humanitarian interests from the threat of ethnic conflict.

Central Asian States

Ethnic Conflict as the Threat to Regional Stability

For illustrative purposes, it might be useful to visualize the following situation:

Today Kazakhstan retaliated on Tashkent, Uzbekistan, with chemical and biological weapons making it a virtual wasteland. Former Soviet scientists inside Kazakhstan developed these weapons, under loose governmental control, in former Soviet laboratories. The attack was in response to Uzbekistan's expulsion and slaughter of thousands of ethnic Kazakhs within its borders and the destruction of 50 miles of the priceless oil pipeline that has fueled Kazakhstan's economic expansion. As a member of the Common-

wealth of Independent States (CIS) Security Arrangement, Kazakhstan will bring Russian forces into the
region. On the other side, as the seventh largest producer of uranium and with the world's 15th largest
energy reserves, Uzbek leaders expect Chinese and
Western backing. Could leaders have foreseen this es-
calation from ethnic violence to global involvement?

Although this scenario is not going to occur this year,
this situation and CENTCOM's preparedness to fulfill its
national military strategy (NMS) roles of "shaping, responding, and preparing now" for this scenario are topics
that cry for attention. Ethnic conflict—long misunder-
stood—has been the root of many crises over the past
decade involving United Nations (UN), North Atlantic
Treaty Organization (NATO), and US forces. Today, there
are more than 35 ongoing conflicts, with more than one-
half being ethnically driven. These civil wars, as one study
concluded, have made up 10 of the 13 "most deadly conflicts" of the nineteenth and twentieth centuries.[1]

Ethnic conflict in this region presents specific political
and military challenges, which include interrelated domestic policies, significant foreign influence, and the newness
of these states. For the US military, challenges include former Soviet training, equipment, doctrine, the nature of
ethnic conflict, and the geographic context of the CAS. But
the stakes are high and CENTCOM must be ready through
preparation and, more importantly, an enhanced understanding of the threat posed by ethnic conflict—this understanding should have a starting point.

Defining Ethnic Conflict Historically

The following definition provides this starting point.
"Ethnic conflict is defined in terms of political, social, or
military confrontation, violent and non-violent, in which
the disputants describe themselves in terms of race, language, religion, culture, or nationality or some combina-
tion of ascriptive criteria."[2]

From the Mongol invasions of Central Asia to the Soviet
conquests of this region, political change has most often been
implemented through violence. These violent changes were

based on religion, nationality, ethnicity, or just pure conquest. Clashes between cultures and societies created the extremely complicated ethnic groups which exist in Central Asia today. For example, the Kazakhs started as a nomadic Turkic people but later converted to Sunni Muslims after Genghis Khan conquered them in the thirteenth century.[3] In the 1700s Cossacks dominated the region, and by 1885 Czar Alexander III's Russian (Orthodox) Empire controlled all of Central Asia.[4] By destroying their religious practices, their assets, and their mobility, the Bolsheviks made the union ruinous for Kazakhs by 1920.[5] This is but one example of the complex history of the current ethnic situation in Central Asia. The common thread throughout the region is the aspect of Soviet dominance and Soviet-style policies through most of the twentieth century.

The era of Soviet domination provided this multiethnic region with three essential elements: political stability, security for all ethnic groups, and—most importantly—a relatively predictable future. The Soviets used immigration and ethnic resettlement as tools to maintain the balance of power within the region in much the same way as many dictators, which limited the power of any one ethnic group while dampening ethnic tensions within the now interdependent groups. But as in the former Yugoslavia, the dissolution of the Soviet Union erased this interdependence and eliminated the three elements that Soviet communism had brought. Thus, today's ethnic problems are caused by the removal of hard-line communism, which has unlocked "ancient hatreds"—or has it?

According to David A. Lake and Donald Rothchild, this common deduction is false:

> Ethnic conflict is not caused by inter-group differences, "ancient hatreds," or the stresses of modern life within a global economy. Nor did the end of the Cold War simply uncork ethnic passions long-bottled up by repressive communist regimes. Rather, ethnic conflict is caused by collective fears for the future. Instead ethnic conflict often takes root as groups begin to fear for their physical safety, and a series of dangerous and difficult to resolve strategic dilemmas arise that contain within them the potential for tremendous violence.[6]

Revisiting the three concepts brought by Soviet control—political stability, security, and predictable futures—a situation "ripe" for ethnic conflict has developed. What factors serve as the triggers or proximate causes for these conflicts? Michael E. Brown—an expert on the nature of war—suggests that there are four possible causes: bad leaders, bad domestic problems, bad neighbors, and bad neighborhoods.[7]

Bad Leaders

Most internal conflict is rooted in bad leaders. Of the on-going conflicts, more than 20 were elite-triggered versus seven mass-triggered struggles.[8] These struggles can be categorized as ideological, criminal, or pure power struggles. For instance, the current conflict in Tajikistan is a *power* rather than an *ideological* struggle. In this case unorganized ethnic minorities are vulnerable to scapegoating, ethnic-bashing, and discrimination solely to court the power inherent in the majority. Brown says, "power struggles are most likely to lead to widespread violence when political elites are vulnerable, group histories are antagonistic, and domestic economic problems are mounting."[9] In Tajikistan and throughout the CAS, leaders are suspect in the wisdom of their policies given their ethnic situations. Questionable are the Uzbek and Kazakh presidents who have both mandated single official languages. This may be acceptable in the case of Uzbek-istan's 74 percent ethnic Uzbek population, but is it effective for Kazakhs who only make up roughly 45 percent of their country? In each case, the presidents appear to be wooing the single biggest ethnic groups—those in power within the government. One more complicating factor is that Russians and other minorities provide the scientific and business expertise in these countries. To alienate them through poor leadership will be to drive them out of the country, thereby losing essential natural resources.[10] Unfortunately, bad leaders usually do not operate in a vacuum. Their influence creates bad domestic problems.

Bad Domestic Problems

Domestic problems, specifically economic growth and distribution of wealth, are crucial elements in analyzing internal conflict. Examples such as Finland have proven that for political stability, ethnically homogeneous populations can withstand significant economic downturns without resorting to domestic or internal violence. Conversely, Indonesia and the Ukraine illustrate how multiethnic populations—such as those in the CAS—will tend to remain at peace only as long as there are continued economic benefits in doing so. Succinctly put by Lt Col Forrest Wentworth, Air Command and Staff College instructor: "People focus on how many GI Joes and Barbie dolls they can buy their kids for Christmas, both this year and next, rather than historical hatred."

These GI Joes and Barbie dolls have been increasingly tough to come by in Central Asia. Loss of subsidies from Moscow, government inefficiencies, and a reluctance on the part of foreigners to invest here has made economic growth elusive. So why has there not been large-scale violence? Combining the ideas of Lake and Rothchild's with Wentworth's, the tremendous *potential* for economic growth, particularly energy-based progress, keeps most of the states in balance.

Other domestic issues contributing to the ripeness for conflict in the region include changing demographic patterns, exclusionary national policies, and failure to modernize institutions and industry. Domestic issues shape ethnic group perceptions and expectations for the future. In the CAS these expectations are regional since policies and expectations in any of the individual CAS affect groups throughout the neighborhood. This neighborhood poses unique and dangerous challenges for each of the CAS.

Bad Neighbors and Neighborhoods

There are few more difficult situations than being an NIS situated in the middle of religious, ethnic, and power play areas. Formative governments, exploitable natural resources, low levels of security, and newly acquired freedoms make this entire area attractive for forces both inside the Central Asian neighborhood and bordering it.

Starting from the north, the Russians have exerted pressure to maintain the CIS Security Arrangement and have managed to keep all but Uzbekistan within its framework. Russian influence or lack of decisive intervention has, in most opinions, kept the civil war in Tajikistan going.[11] Kazakh concern that its Russian minority was susceptible to breakaway tendencies was so strong that they moved their capital hundreds of miles north from Almaty to Astana, in a "flag-planting" maneuver.

Moving east, Turkish influence of their ethnically related brothers has been moderated by a weak Turkish economy, their own ethnic problems with Kurds and Bulgars, and their preoccupation with the European Union. Graham Fuller, a political scientist at RAND, states

> A strengthening in nationalist forces within Central Asia will benefit Turkey. Over the long run, Turkish influence will probably increase rather than decrease. For this reason it is expected that Turkey can be expected to play a stronger role in democratization in the region in the expectation that it will lead to greater Turkish influence as nationalists have a chance to gain power.[12]

This relationship has been significantly enhanced by the recent agreements on oil pipelines.

Continuing to the south, Iranian influence, strongest in Turkmenistan and Tajikistan, has had limited success. An important concept often overlooked is the fact that Iran and Pakistan are mainly Shia Muslim—a sect that promotes fundamentalism—whereas, Saudi Arabia, Turkey, and the majority of NIS are Sunni Muslim—a sect that tends toward secularism in government. These forces counterbalance each other. Iranian interests here include the division of the Caspian Sea and oil pipeline projects. With Iran distracted by current government unrest between its supreme leader and president, Mujahadeen-e-Khalk attacks, and its immediate concerns in Afghanistan, it has had little time to devote in exporting fundamentalism to the CAS.[13] Some believe that once Iran's current regime is stabilized, its influence will be tied to that of Iraq. In the scenario where Iraq is dismembered or crippled by American efforts, Iran will concentrate on expanding its influence in the north, thus prompting possible Russian retaliation.[14] With that said, Russian voting patterns regarding UN sanctions on Iraq can be better understood by CENTCOM as voting for their interests rather than voting against ours. This sustains political room for maneuver and military cooperation in the region.

Afghan and Pakistani borders bound the southeast CAS. Although the self-proclaimed Taliban supported by the Pakistanis remains a source of fundamentalism in Tajikistan, the legitimate Afghan government group—lodged in the Ferghana Valley—is their dominant concern.[15] Significant issues in this part of the neighborhood include porous borders allowing sanctuary, insurgent infiltration routes, arms trade, and drug routes. A glaring example of this is in the Uzbek foreign minister's recent revelation that 400 Uzbek and Tajik guerrillas were trained in Afghan and Pakistani training camps and then infiltrated into Uzbekistan via Kyrgyzstan and Tajikistan.[16]

Moving eastward, China—particularly the Xinjiang province—shores up the last boundary of the neighborhood. This province shapes Kazakh opinion on China, as it once was a Turkic Mongol independent culture and is ethnically similar to other CAS with its Uighers.[17] Although the Chinese province presents economic opportunities, it also resurrects Kazakh fears of Chinese expansionism and religious oppression. Contention for Chinese influence here is undoubtedly based in economics but may be rooted in their desire to maintain a western lever against the underbelly of Russia.

The neighbors have been cooperative with each other thus far, especially those rooted in the ancient Ferghana Valley.[18] Treaties of eternal friendship between Uzbekistan, Kazakhstan, Kyrgyzstan, the Shanghai Five (Russia–China–Kazakhstan–Kyrgyzstan–Tajikistan), CIS, and NATO's Partnership for Peace (PFP) operations illustrate varying degrees of CAS interdependence. These bonds, however, are showing signs of weakness. The *Humanitarian Times* reports "For the Ferghana valley's highly integrated regional economy, the policies implemented by the three governments have had a detrimental impact. Customs controls, establishment of separate currencies and differences in rates and means of economic liberalization tear at the fabric which has woven the Valley together over centuries."[19] Essentially, the neighborhood has remained porous yet respectful of diasporas located within each other's sovereign borders. What happens when this changes?

Ethnic Composition and Diasporas

Diasporas—or ethnic groups trapped or dispersed inside another country—have historically been the scapegoats for violence like Hitler's *Anschluss* (the union with Nazi Germany imposed on Austria by Hitler, with considerable assistance from the Austrians) policy, Soviet action in Poland, and even French involvement in Algeria. This region—ethnically composed by the Soviets—is incredibly susceptible to nationalist leaders who would try to rescue their trapped countrymen in a neighboring state (see appendix A). Stephen Van Evera, from the Massachusetts Institute of Technology's Security Studies Program, notes that "Minority oppressing nationalism can cause war in two ways: by provoking secessions by its captive nations, or spurring the homelands of these captive nations to move forcefully to free their oppressed co-nationals. [This] is most dangerous if the oppressed minorities have nearby friends who have the capacity to protect the oppressed nation by force."[20] From the discussions earlier, every nation in the CAS seems to have a friend to back them up. The weight of these friends and the likelihood of their involvement in an ever-expanding conflict makes CENTCOM's success here crucial.

Why This Spells Bad News

The first report, "New World Coming," of the US Commission on National Security/21st Century (also known as the Hart–Rudman Commission) foresees "An increase in the rise of suppressed nationalism, ethnic or religious violence, humanitarian disasters, major catalytic regional crises, and the spread of dangerous weapons. Most violence will erupt due to internal conflicts in existing states. As more and more people learn about the state of life in the rest of the world they will be less tolerant of their own oppressive or incompetent leaders."[21] The Hart–Rudman Commission's documented projections for conflict in the ensuing 25 years reflect problems related to Central Asia as well as the possibility of US intervention in that region. As a matter of fact, more than one-half of the 14 basic conclusions apply to the US view of Central Asia:

- Rapid advances in information/biotechnology will create new vulnerabilities for US security.

- New technologies will divide the world as well as draw it together.

- Energy will continue to have major strategic significance.

- All borders will be more porous; some will bend and others will break.

- The sovereignty of states will come under pressure but will endure.

- Fragmentation/failure of states will occur, with destabilizing effects on neighboring states.

- Foreign crises will be replete with atrocities and the terrorizing of civilian populations.

- The essence of war will not change.

- Intelligence will face more challenging adversaries, and excellent intelligence will not prevent surprises.

- The United States will be called upon frequently to intervene militarily in a time of uncertain alliances and with the prospect of fewer forward-deployed forces.

- The emerging security environment in the next quarter century will require different military and other national capabilities.[22]

So what is the most likely direction conflict will take in Central Asia? The primary source of conflict will be ethnic conflict generated from spillover from neighboring CAS. The porous bending and breaking described by the Hart–Rudman Commission allows tremendous political, religious, and military influence to transcend borders. The Afghan and Tajik refugee problems present examples where pressure and demographic balances in certain pockets are changing, leading to the majority's widening fears as to the security of their future.

Spillover from neighboring countries here is inevitable unless all these states can effectively seal their borders. Although a daunting task, the cost of failure to do so may be national survival itself. Brown uses a 1970 example to illustrate. Here, King Hussein I expelled radical Palestinians from Jordan, with most resettling in Lebanon where Christian–Muslim tensions were already mounting. These fighters, mixed with refugees, may have been the sparks that triggered the start of the Lebanese civil war.[23] More recently, US concern for the allocation of Albanian Kosovar refugees proves that they are using lessons learned. Effective border control is a tool to diffuse potential ethnic spillover and can become a means to prevent violence.

In "Hypotheses on Nationalism and War," Van Evera notes that the potential for nationalistic conflict between states can be checked partly by looking at the defensibility of one's borders, their international legitimacy, and the degree of correspondence between political and ethnic boundaries.[24] These three characteristics immediately sound the warning horn in Central Asia. First, as seen by the number of conquerors in this region, the borders of any of these five countries can be defined as indefensible. This fact tends to lead to the conclusion that all of the countries should feel insecure. But taking Van Evera's comments one step further, it may lead all of them to feel more secure since they all have vulnerabilities similar in nature. These security dilemmas could raise tensions in the region if one of the states develops an unmatched military capability. Second, international legitimacy can be illustrated in the Rand–McNally map denoting "Border in Dispute with China" throughout the area. Significant steps have been taken to eliminate this problem, and there are currently no boundary disputes between the five nations. Third, corresponding ethnic and political boundaries have historically caused ethnic conflict. Specifically, African decolonializing this century has seen widespread ethnic violence caused by the European created border demarcations. Unmatched tribal and geographic boundaries triggered internal ethnic conflict and spillover from their diasporas in the neighboring countries. Theorist Samuel P. Huntington describes these lines as cultural "fault lines" around which the world is built. He states that fault lines that run through countries rather than along their political borders create torn countries that have traditionally been ripe for conflict. Due to the nomadic nature of the Central Asian peoples, the fault line has to be based on the boundary of Orthodox and Muslim influence.[25] But as ethnic Russians and Germans repatriate, this fault line shifts northward even though political borders are not changing. Unlike the results of poor line correlation in west Africa, Van Evera observes that "the peaceful dissolution of the former Soviet Union was thus a mixed blessing: its successor states emerged without violence, but with borders that captured unhappy diasporas behind them."[26] In a few cases, especially in Kyrgyzstan and Uzbekistan, small enclaves or autonomous regions have been developed for these "captured" diasporas. Unsettling, though, is the fact that there are no Russian enclaves. This may reinforce Russian minority fears for their future.

In summary, this region has all the elements that have historically caused ethnic conflict. Indeed some authors say that the "complex problems of the Caspian Region could, if left to fester, make the Balkans look like a pregame warm-up."[27] CENTCOM decision makers must understand this context to be able to analyze and operate in this complex but valuable region.

Framing the Context: Identifying US Interests

Our nation's central challenge—and our responsibility—is to sustain the role of the world's most powerful force for peace, prosperity, and the universal values of democracy and freedom by seizing opportunities of this new global era for the benefit of our own people and people around the world.

—A National Security Strategy for a New Century

To analyze the importance of Central Asia with regard to US interests, the starting point must be national policies. This section discusses stated interests in the CAS focusing on WMD, natural resources, drug smuggling, US influence and credibility, and humanitarian issues.

Current National Security Strategy

The national security strategy (NSS) stratifies US interests into three broad categories: vital, important, and humanitarian and other interests. A quick review of these will help frame the CAS.

Vital Interests

Vital interests are defined as broad, overriding importance to the survival, safety, and vitality of our nation.[28] They include the following:

- physical security of our territory and that of our allies,

- the safety of our citizens,

- the economic well-being of our society, and

- the protection of critical infrastructures from paralyzing attack.

The vital interests in this region include WMD, terrorists, and the immense strategic resources of the CAS (e.g., oil, natural gas, uranium, etc.).

Important Interests

These interests do not affect our national survival, but rather our national well-being and the character of the world in which we live.[29] Defined in this manner, important interests include

- regions in which we have a sizable economic stake or commitments to allies,

- protecting the global environment from severe harm, and

- crises with a potential to generate substantial and highly destabilizing refugee flows.

Important US interests in the CAS are drug trafficking, civil wars in Afghanistan and Tajikistan, and Iranian influence.[30]

Humanitarian and Other Interests

Acting because our values demand it, these tertiary interests may be framed as:

- response to natural and man-made disasters,

- promoting human rights and seeking halts to gross violations of those rights,

- supporting democratization,

- adherence to the rule of law and civilian control of the military,

- assistance in humanitarian demining, and

- promoting sustainable development and environmental protection.[31]

US interests that fall into this category include disaster preparedness, democratic reform, legal reform, the inclusion of the NIS into the World Trade Organization (WTO) and US/foreign investment.[32]

Weapons of Mass Destruction

According to the NSS, WMD poses "the greatest potential threat to global stability and security."[33] Although 1995 marked the establishment of the Central Asian Nuclear Weapons Free Zone, security at previous nuclear, biological, and chemical laboratories and the whereabouts of their resident experts have come into question. Ethnic conflict, the resulting government destabilization, and lax security could mean a fire sale of deadly weapons and materials for any entity hostile to the United States and its allies. Once in possession of WMD, groups mired in a fight for their sheer existence may use the materials in numerous ways to:

- direct use on the opposing ethnic groups or ruling government,

- threaten WMD use as a deterrent for international intervention,

- use or threaten use of WMD internationally as a cry for intervention,

- sell the material to finance their struggle because they have no means of application, and

- serve as a transit route (safer than Europe) for smuggled Russian WMD material.

From the CAS government side of the equation, there is a potential win-win situation for the regimes. Getting rid of the WMD and the capability to produce such materials is unquestionably in the CAS's best interest. Since the price CAS governments would pay for using these weapons is prohibitively high, they might as well get the most out of discarding them.

Use or threatened use of these weapons by legitimate governments would promote international alienation much like it did with Iraqi chemical attacks in the 1980s. In these developing states, positive international attention replete with economic and diplomatic benefits remains a necessity. Any form of sanctions would crush economic growth, thus exacerbating hopes for a brighter future. Currently, sanctions and US policy on Tajikistan have limited US military engagement there, thus reducing shaping options.

WMD use by government forces on any specific ethnic group, regardless of insurgent identity, would tend to escalate neighboring countries' concerns for their diasporas. These types of atrocities and their tremendous killing capability would demand quick military responses from their protectorate nations before their entire diaspora was exterminated.

The most likely step for the current regimes is selling the material for nation-building funds. Unfortunately, current intelligence cannot identify all of the buyers; and the US pullout and sanctioning of Tajikistan and Kazakhstan created intelligence shortfalls in this subject. Of the two countries, Kazakh WMD capabilities are the most worrisome. The Kazakh regime possesses components of a WMD capability: they control former Soviet laboratories, scientists, fissile material, and production facilities (see appendix B). This is not a country that the United States can afford to disengage. Previous programs administered under the Department of State's (DOS) Cooperative Threat Reduction (CTR) Program have included highly enriched uranium (HEU) buys, the funding of relocations of scientists to the United States, and enhanced security protection measures. All of these are profitable endeavors for the countries involved.[34]

The real possibility of the CAS being a transit route from Russia to the Middle East or South Asia can present terrible consequences for US security. On this issue the problems lie with porous borders and total disengagement in the entry and two avenues of exit for the materials. In late 1999 the United States suspended relations with Kazakhstan due to the sale of MiG-21s to North Korea. Although the delivery was turned around and the personnel were recently tried and imprisoned, CENTCOM's ability to engage here remains on hold.[35] This attitude reduces our shaping options, strains our intelligence capabilities, and reduces US credibility in this first stop of WMD material out of Russia. US isolation of Tajikistan also allows the trade route to continue unimpeded with possible outlets into China, Pakistan, Afghanistan, and Iran. Of those, lack of US engagement in all but China allows little involvement or interdiction along this WMD smuggling route. Additionally, without US economic involvement in these countries, what profession would bring more money than WMD smuggling? What is the risk-reward equation in life and resources of an Iranian WMD threat versus the cost of the US normalization of diplomatic ties? Although changing current US policy is beyond the purview of the military, DOS and the Department of Defense (DOD) should consider two significant factors: MiG-21s that never made it to their destination are far easier to defend against than a WMD device obtained in Kazakhstan, and the military's ability to engage in the region depends on on-scene intelligence and good relationships between US forces and the host nation. Allowing CENTCOM activities to resume in Kazakhstan and Tajikistan enables an effective arm of American influence. That influence is not only focused on defending the United States and our allies but also on promoting US prosperity.

Resources

We are focusing particular attention on investment in Caspian energy resources and their export from the region to world markets, thereby expanding and diversifying world energy supplies and promoting prosperity in the region. Development of Caspian energy resources will improve our energy security.

—*A National Security Strategy for a New Century*

Energy resources in this area are staggering. Comparable in quantity to US and North Sea oil reserves, Caspian

Sea reserves exist mostly offshore and remain unexplored. Even more impressive are the natural gas possibilities. Looking at proven reserves, Kazakhstan, Turkmenistan, and Uzbekistan each rank among the world's 20 largest natural gas countries and match North America's tremendous reserves.[36]

Two positive effects of these resources exist. First, the abundant resources—given a stable and beneficial price of crude oil—contribute to economic development, enhancing prosperity and stability. Second, there is regional unity on both sides of the Caspian due to interconnecting production and transporting mechanisms. However, there are also two possible negatives associated with these resources. First, the imbalance of wealth among the CAS—based on petroleum revenues—will tend to alienate Kyrgyzstan and Tajikistan and will make the vision of a unified economic region difficult. Currently, Kyrgyzstan overcomes the appearance of the laggard by maintaining the fastest pace in economic reforms and the lead in industry, hydroelectric power, and water resources. Kyrgyzstan could be locked into the future of the region with an investment in refining technology or could become a crucial route in pipelines taking oil and gas to China. The second negative is the attention of having resources that everyone wants. Powerful forces from the United States, Russia, China, Iran, Turkey, and multinational energy companies have increased the choices available for Caspian region governments. The gravity of decisions regarding what routes to traverse and where to drill for these resources has implications for US and allied national security. For the United States, these specifics present strategic centers of gravity that must be defended.

Oil and Natural Gas

For years Middle Eastern countries have projected their defense buildups and social programs based on crude oil prices per barrel. Until recently, the Organization of Petroleum Exporting Countries (OPEC) surpluses, a slowing rate of energy consumption, and other energy markets have kept the price of oil below the targets that would create the defense budgets of a regional military giant. In fact, even if the recent upsurge of crude prices continues, it will probably take years to erase the debts accrued during the 1990s. During this time, the United States may continue to be the dominant source of defense and security for the region. Aside from the defense issues, another problem is the stymied growth of these oil-rich states.

But the future looks bright. Since independence the CAS has moved to achieve economic prosperity built on energy revenues. Making energy their priority, Uzbekistan and Turkmenistan have increased their oil production significantly.[37] One underperformer, Kazakhstan, has seen a slump in production and slower than expected exploitation of its offshore potential.[38] Overall, combined 1997 CAS oil production from the Caspian was respectable but still dwarfed by OPEC leaders like Saudi Arabia and Iran (see table 1). Essential to US national security, extra producers help stabilize world markets through increased market competition and expanded choices.[39]

Table 1

CAS Oil and Gas Statistics

Producer	Total Oil Reserves	Total Oil Production	Total Gas Reserves	Total Gas Production
Iran*	12 BBL	N/A	0 Tcf	0 Bcf
Russia	5 BBL	60,000 BL	N/A	N/A
Kazakhstan	95–103 BBL	573,300 BL	53–83 Tcf	215.4 Bcf
Turkmenistan	34 BBL	107,300 BL	98–155 Tcf	610.9 Bcf
Uzbekistan	1 BBL	182,400 BL	74–88 Tcf	1,808.1 Bcf

BBL = billion barrels
BL = barrels per day
Tcf = trillion cubic feet
Bcf = billion cubic feet per year

*Iranian values only reflect oil and natural gas from the Iranian section of the Caspian Sea.

Source: On-line, Internet, 5 January 2000, available from http://www.eia.doe.gov/emeu/lpsr/t12.txt.

CAS natural gas looks similar, again with Uzbekistan the standout in production increases. Crippled with Russian bureaucratic links, Kazakh natural gas production is not near its potential. Similarly, Turkmenistan, with the world's third largest proven natural gas reserves—until recently tied to Russian transport methods—has not even begun any form of exploration. Uzbekistan, on the other hand, has become the world's eighth largest producer through active production and exploration.[40] These illustrate some but not all of the problems with getting to the reserves.

Another major issue confronting the CAS is the transportation and refining aspects of the energy market. Until recently, privatized Russian firms like Gazprom and Lukezoil have monopolized energy through previous refining agreements and tremendous transport and conversion fees. With increased international attention and significant investment by the major oil companies, CAS oil producers have begun to learn the intricacies of international free markets. Many of the state-run oil, gas, coal, and mineral companies have already privatized or formed joint ventures with Western or Middle Eastern firms.[41] Still, these are limited facilities, both in number of plants and in production capacities.[42] Overall, this region and the stability of its economies will take off provided there is guaranteed security of the system and improvements in the production and distribution systems (see appendix C). But oil and gas are not the only assets in Central Asia.

Strategic Minerals

The last of the resources that bear on the strategic nature of the region is uranium. It is found in significant quantity in Uzbekistan and Kazakhstan. Specifically, Uzbekistan is the seventh largest uranium producer, producing more than 5 percent of world output with plans to double that by the end of 2000.[43] This is a staggering statistic, but it is overshadowed by the fact that both nations possess the ability to make their raw uranium into weapons grade or HEU.[44] Since 1991 DOS purchases of HEU through CTR funds have been significant. The United States needs to understand that it cannot buy 38,000 metric tons and should instead focus on the dismantling of the HEU process that actually makes the resource militarily relevant.

Implications for Future Conflict

So what could ethnic conflict have to do with natural resources? There are three main dynamics or outcomes that should be considered in regards to a continued stable production of CAS energy resources.

First, as mentioned earlier, other states in the region may feel threatened by a rich neighbor. Unless oil-rich CAS find ways to include their poorer neighbors and thus different ethnic groups through joint ventures or a regional profit-sharing structure, there is a great possibility of this resource imbalance creating a security dilemma. Surely, the oil-rich nations will feel the need to protect their borders, energy industries, and cultures. Buying arms to do so may be perceived as the precursor to an arms race that the others would have to match or counter through strategic alliances. Some of the agreements discussed earlier—such as the Uzbek–Kyrg–Kazakh eternal friendship declaration and the CIS security arrangement—make great strides in limiting this effect. US decisions regarding military aid should consider this effect very seriously.

Second, ethnic conflict caused by spillover would involve guerrilla forces operating outside one country and striking targets within another. An oil-dependent CAS would be a tremendous target for guerrillas. The asymmetry of a small band destroying or holding hostage a refinery or a key pipeline would be catastrophic for any of the three oil-producing nations.

Third, with so many outside entities interested in the energy resources in the region, foreign governments may be quicker to intervene in unstable situations—basing their justification on ethnicity rather than their interest in energy. Governments interested in either disrupting or destroying oil production in the region may also use ethnic conflict as a means to introduce agents or insurgents to do their "dirty work." Likely suspects would be the contenders for energy dominance in the region such as Iran and other Caspian Sea players. In constructive moves the United

States has announced backing for many projects that create interdependent relations—for example, pipelines from Turkmenistan to Turkey and Uzbekistan to Azerbaijan that will dampen animosity between Caspian region producers. Currently, the main issue between the Trans–Caspian nations is the actual post–Soviet-era division of the Caspian and ownership of offshore drilling and exploration areas. This issue, although divisive, has not resulted in violence or subversion by any Caspian players. These energy and minerals are tangible interests in Central Asia.

Influence and Credibility

US engagement in Central Asia is a security imperative. Encouraging stability and integration of the CAS into world political and economic organizations only strengthens US security.[45] Examples of this are evident in the successful American backing of Kyrgyzstan into the WTO and the integration of all five countries into NATO's PFP program.[46] All of the CAS are currently members of the Organization for Security and Cooperation in Europe and have welcomed their participation in election monitoring.[47]

The Shanghai Five and the CIS security arrangements are organizations that can be interpreted many ways in terms of US security. First, the Shanghai Five feels that they dominate the Central Asian landscape; thus, they feel secure against US intervention in the region. They also stabilize the region since it combines China and Russia into a single powerful group. Other alliances like the informal agreements between Iran and China tend to counterbalance possible Russian adventurism in the name of helping ethnic Russians. The CIS security arrangement seems to have a stabilizing effect in these developing nations by providing time for nation-building. As seen in Vietnam, there was no "winning the hearts and minds" of the populace by the US Operations Mission or US Military Assistance Programs without the element of security.[48] The last dynamic, Iranian–Russian relations, centers around Iranian "direct dialogue with Moscow about their mutual interest in preventing the Turks from making greater inroads into Central Asia."[49]

US influence in the region is hampered by access to the area and, in some cases, failure to engage. World opinion on US credibility is always at stake in situations from which the United States disengages, especially if ethnic conflict or the perception of ethnic-based conflict is present. Abroad, US activities in backing Israeli policies in southern Lebanon can be perceived as hypocritical when measured against US lack of action in the Islamic fundamentalists versus the secularists in this region. US sanctions on Kazakhstan for a sale of virtually insignificant MiG-21s to North Korea may contrast sharply with US inaction against Israel in response to Patriot technology transfers to Iran. Although many in the CAS are Soviet-era thinkers who see the United States as the entity who forced them to endure the Soviet leadership's demands for more production and less freedom, most nations and their media are reportedly pro-West.[50] They strive to gain access to Western markets, consumer goods, and freedoms. This is America's chance to give it to them. In return, the United States will build credibility and influence while enhancing US and CAS security against threats like the transnational issue of drug smuggling.

Drug Smuggling

Since Afghan "freedom fighters" supposedly financed their struggle with drug money, it would not be surprising that CAS insurgents would do the same. Ethnic Uzbek insurgents, Tajik fighters, and Islamic fundamentalists are profiting from poor border security, economic conditions, and growing world demand for illegal drugs. This demand takes Central/South Asian cannabis, opium, and heroin and distributes it into Russia/Western Europe.[51] Since devout Muslims do not use drugs, CAS drugs are similar to oil resources—they remain totally dependent on successful transport onto world markets. In essence, lax border security and corruption means that a tremendous amount of illegal drugs and dollars enter Russia, destabilizing an economy that the United States and the International Monetary Fund are keeping afloat.

The US Drug Enforcement Agency's new field office in Uzbekistan suggests that a significant amount of drugs moves through the region.[52] The Afghan lesson taught Tajiks that through eradication the government could deny opium profits to insurgents in their Khulyabi–Khojand civil war.[53] In the long run, failure to aid CAS governments in this mission and border issues means that all US instruments of power will cost more and take longer to achieve the desired effect against movements or ethnic groups that are well armed and financed. Those well-armed groups can also turn an illegal drug trade into ethnic conflict and a humanitarian nightmare.

Humanitarian Tragedy/EthnicCleansing

Seen in the Balkans and Central Africa, humanitarian tragedies such as ethnic cleansing present the United States with difficult choices. Although US leaders tend to base their involvement on the Weinberger–Powell principles, the immense public outcry "to do something" creates a dangerous condition for prolonged military action. Could ethnic cleansing occur in Central Asia? According to Andrew Bell–Fialkoff, a "cleansing is most likely to occur in situations of (1) sudden reversals of status; (2) loss of social, economic, or political advantages; and (3) the presence of ethnic allies across new borders. Solutions to the problems of cleansing must consider (A) the creation of stable and recognizable borders; (B) a geographic distribution of minorities; (C) numerical strength; and (D) the rate of growth of each ethnic population."[54]

The issue of stable and secure borders is paramount, as is the geographic distribution of minorities. Throughout the CAS, minorities have grouped themselves into tight enclaves that may even speak a different language than their surrounding countrymen. Enclaves like these have been, in some cases, turned into autonomous regions attached to a "mother country." However, the fact that they are numerically strong within a sovereign country makes them vulnerable to majority reprisals like ethnic cleansing. A probable scenario that meets the conditions above would be a sudden shift to fundamentalist governments. This would be a "reversal," definitely a "loss of advantage" to all those outside of the religion. The movement would undoubtedly have "ethnic allies" across their borders. An example "ripe" for an ethnic expulsion is where Uzbekistan's president stated that " 'We do not want an Islamic state as a neighbor.' Tajikistan has taken its Islamic opposition into a coalition government, a move which will inevitably shift the politics of the country and which relieves the Tajik Islamic militants to carry their movement into Uzbekistan [and its 6 percent ethnic Tajik population]."[55]

Overall, ethnic cleansing presents a real problem in terms of the speed of decisions required and then the speed of implementation of any US response. US commitment to action and end states must be considered prior to deployment or even the suggestion of deployment of troops. Unlike Kosovo, the extreme distances, the limited methods of resupply, and the possibility of intervention by more international players will make any hesitation to act a decision in itself.

So what can CENTCOM do? CENTCOM must first understand the context it is operating in, make smart decisions regarding engagement that emphasize regional bonds, and focus on the stated US interests here. The CAS is a valuable region both in payoff and protection, and CENTCOM must take the lead in suggesting options to both defend and promote US interests.

Applying the National Military Strategy: Shaping CENTCOM Strategy

What stands out is just how ineffective the international community has been in imposing a modicum of civility on even those small states one might have thought it was in a position to coerce. Actually when states themselves have taken the initiative, they have done better—which suggests that these domestic problems are best handled domestically, although they are rarely handled well at all.

—Timothy D. Sisk
Power Sharing and International Mediation in Ethnic Conflicts

Derived from the NSS, the NMS outlines the imperatives of military engagement. More clearly, the strategy stresses military roles in terms of *shaping* the international environment, *responding* to a full spectrum of crises, and *preparing now* for an uncertain future.[56] In each case, military engagement requires commitment and perseverance for success. This commitment must be across the entire spectrum of the national instruments of power (IOP). In diplomatic situations like Tajikistan and Kazakhstan where the DOD is not engaged, the DOS loses the leverage of military funding, manpower, and materiel in shaping the environment. Regardless of how much preparation a commander in chief (CINC) may do, the respond phase—which may have been avoidable—may now be more costly in terms of US lives and resources than if the military was fully engaged in shaping from the start.

CENTCOM Specifics

Transferred from the Joint Chiefs of Staff to CENTCOM, the CAS presents unique challenges. Some of the most pronounced ethnic tensions—coupled with historical animosity, international power plays, and abundant WMD facilities situated in a resource rich, underdeveloped region—make it imperative that CENTCOM develop a successful strategy for Central Asia. Unfortunately, the resources have not come along with this need. According to Maj Steven Latchford, two personnel billets and only a modest increase in traditional CINC activities funds transferred with this five-nation responsibility. Luckily, National Guard Bureau (NGB) country programs (see table 2) developed in the early 1990s absorbed some of the shortfall through military-military contact and educational visits. Future CENTCOM operations in the region will have to make the most out of well-informed planning and interagency cooperation, specifically with the US Agency for International Development (USAID) to be exact. DOS CTR funds and USAID's democracy program—along with NGB and CENTCOM dollars—may mean a successful, stable Central Asia free to develop its own economy and democracies.

Table 2

National Guard Partnerships with Central Asian States

National Guard	Partner Country
Arizona	Kazakhstan
Louisiana	Uzbekistan
Montana	Kyrgyzstan
Nevada	Turkmenistan

Source: "National Guard Bureau International Affairs Central Command Theater Overview," n.p., on-line, Internet, 30 December 1999, available from http://www. ngb.dtic.mil/bureau/ochief/ia/centcom_ovrview1.html.

Shaping the International Environment

CENTCOM's role in shaping the CAS includes promoting stability, preventing or reducing conflicts, and peacetime deterrence. Shaping sets the stage for future operations and can lay the foundation for whether insurgencies will occur. As Max Manwaring points out:

> The ultimate outcome of any counterinsurgency effort is not primarily determined by the skillful manipulation of violence in many military battles. Rather the outcome will be determined by the *legitimacy of the government, organization for unity of effort, type and consistency of support for the targeted government, ability to reduce outside aid to the insurgents, intelligence (or action against subversion), and discipline and capabilities of a government's armed forces.* The elements of this paradigm are not culturally bound in terms of Western values and goals. The paradigm can help to explain the dynamics of low intensity conflict not only in traditional and modernizing societies but also in industrial states facing the monumental changes unleashed by the breakdown of the former Soviet Empire (emphasis added).[57]

Taking each one of these presents ideas for CENTCOM's role in shaping the environment (see table 3).

Military-to-Military Contacts (Effective)

CENTCOM contacts range from CINC and senior DOD country visits to US Military and Naval Academy tours for CAS armed forces. This approach enhances legitimacy of the governments while displaying US commitment to the region. US contact visits should be coordinated with DOS activities and across the interagency and joint military

Table 3
CENTCOM Program Ratings Overview

Activity	Rating*
Military-to-Military Contacts	Effective
Theater Engagement Planning Management Information System (TEPMIS)	Very Effective
Foreign Military Sales/Excess Defense Articles (FMS/EDA)	Somewhat Effective
Education	Effective
Military Exercises	Somewhat Effective
Other Shaping Activities	Somewhat Effective

*The rating system is based on both potential—if the fixes are implemented (e.g., TEPMIS)—and current (e.g., FMS/EDA) which provides minimal aid without a strategy.

spectrums. CAS visits should begin to stress "Central Asia a regional fighting unit" by grouping low-level visits together. A commander (J-7) described this type of contact as a "cheap way to enhance learning and provide a forum for sharing perspectives."[58]

Theater Engagement Planning Management and Information System (Very Effective)

TEPMIS is an excellent single source for managing and maintaining visibility into all of the organizations and activities in CENTCOM's area of responsibility (AOR). This allows all agencies to build on other activities, enhances unity of effort in the region, and allows CINCCENTCOM to better visualize engagement strategy. The program's main shortfall is the lack of accountability for database entries that could make this tool outdated or irrelevant. CINC-CENTCOM should assign responsibility for updates and continue funding and integration of TEPMIS.

Foreign Military Sales/ExcessDefense Articles (Somewhat Effective)

FMS/EDA programs for the CAS appear to be inadequate, totally reactionary, and disjointed. Determining CAS needs—especially in border control, protection of high-value facilities like oil refineries and pipelines, and maritime self-defense—should be the main focus of FMS/EDA programs. Analyzing EDA for the type and consistency of support for a targeted government rather than a reactive response to CAS requests is the strategy of shaping. Problems that have slowed EDA programs—such as CAS defense structure and funding to get the materiel to the region—should be solved in standing agreements with DOS rather than reactive negotiations. Although the temptation in EDA would be to provide the bulk to "jewels of Central Asia" Kazakhstan and Uzbekistan, careful consideration should be given to the effects on the earlier discussed balances of power. FMS/EDA should focus on the asymmetric nature of possible ethnic conflict by focusing on border security equipment and rapid response capabilities (i.e., troops transport via helicopters and fast coastal patrol boats). Trends should also steer the CAS towards US–NATO interoperability (i.e., communications, identification friend or foe equipment, etc.) enhancing both the payoffs at PFP exercises and future training opportunities.

Education (Effective)

Prior to full CENTCOM engagement, some CAS students who were to attend two-month Professional Military Education (PME) courses would spend one year in the United States learning English.[59] Positive investment in language laboratories in each of the CAS is paying off. Continued investment in this area will make all other individual military education and training (IMET) programs possible. IMET funding for humanitarian assistance and field medicine courses has been a success for the Arizona National Guard. Members from all CAS are scheduled for their courses, once again promoting regional as well as US–CAS unity.

Since all CAS nations deploy peacekeepers to Tajikistan, a superb idea would be US funding of UN peacekeeping courses for CAS participants.[60] Again, legal issues stand in the way. IMET money must not be used to pay for foreign military attendance at foreign schools. Dialogue with the sometimes free Nordic UN peacekeeping courses can make CAS participation a reality. Continued efforts to send leaders to courses at the Marshall Center, senior and midlevel military PME courses, and noncommissioned officer courses will enhance members' understanding of the proper civil-military relations. The desired PME end state should be a regional course within the CAS. With the unhealthy trend of ethnically centered state militaries in the CAS, militaries must be unquestionably professional and respectful of both military and civilian minorities. A possible way to reduce the apprehension of ethnic minorities in the military is through leadership courses, awards, and promotion systems based on US models and taught in US PME. To combat the growing sophistication of transnational actors, more technical IMET programs such as the US Marine Corps's (USMC) border patrol, military operations in urban terrain (MOUT), and chemical and biological hazard training is mandatory. US Army helicopter training, Special Forces, and US Coast Guard (USCG) courses also are programs that will enhance CAS military capabilities to employ effectively our EDA materiel (i.e., UH-60 Blackhawks and USCG patrol boats).[61]

Military Exercises (Somewhat Effective)

Although Central Asian States Battalion 2000 involves most of the CAS, it needs to evolve into a quarterly event. Effective in rapid reaction, airdrop, and tactical maneuver training, CENTCOM should also use Central Asia to enhance all US and CAS capabilities in MOUT, mountain operations, and WMD handling. The regional approach allows a single vision to be broadcast and sends the message that the United States intends to support all of them.

Other Shaping Activities (Somewhat Effective)

The US Army's Corps of Engineers project targeting both military undertakings (especially improvement of airfields and transportation infrastructure) and civil undertakings that can create both capability and credibility for future CENTCOM operations. In shaping the WMD realm, CENTCOM must work more closely in conjunction with the Departments of Energy and State. Enticing more former Soviet scientists and continuing HEU buys with CTR funds remain vital activities. Possibly as training missions, securing, inspecting, and installing monitoring devices at the major WMD plants (i.e., Vozrozhdenly Island—see appendix B) and military medical responses to WMD events enhance US security.

Drug and technology smuggling must be combated by an active border control strategy. Ongoing work with the Nonproliferation Division of DOS, the Drug Enforcement Administration, and Central Intelligence Agency will create enhanced border control measures and enforcement techniques for the region. This not only reduces direct threats to US and allied security but also limits the possibility of spillover of ethnic violence on a given country. All of these are shaping strategies that will be cheaper and more effective in protecting US goals than having to respond militarily.

Responding to the Full Spectrum of Crises

The fight in Central Asia will entail the deployment, engagement, or containment of warring parties, as well as conflict termination and resolution. Massive CENTCOM resources will be needed to develop—as the end state—a stable, prosperous region that bolsters potential US economic prosperity and respects the democratic rights of all of its inhabitants. Unfortunately, the infrastructure required for such an operation has neither been planned for nor designed.

Due to geography, CENTCOM operational choices are limited. Quick-reaction, forced-entry capabilities inherent in the USMC and logistics constrain possible operations in Central Asia. Inaccessible to maritime forces, US airlift would bear the brunt of requirements. From "beans to bullets" and the fighting airmen and soldiers, US Transportation Command (USTRANSCOM) would have to use only 25 airfields in the CAS to perform its mission. The maximum on the ground (MOG) issues at these airfields remains a limiting factor that CENTCOM planners should address even in the shaping phase.[62]

Additionally, the "air bridge" to get to Central Asia will be hindered by political constraints. For instance, if CENTCOM planners design routes with Turkish overflight required, then US involvement in the disputed area will have to mirror Turkish interests as well. Greek and Bulgarian or Macedonian and Romanian overflights are other routes that planners may take. Turkish relations with Bulgaria have been rapidly improving, thus making this a vulnerable capability to plan on. Unconventionally, prepositioning airlift in Georgia or other Caspian countries prior to hostilities, shipping men and material through the Bosporous Strait to that country and then airlifting them to the CAS is a workable, but inefficient, method of global reach. In any case, once in the CAS, individual states may deny overflight in step with their CIS security arrangement. The bottom line for preparing and conducting a fight in the CAS is that it will be politically constrained and nearly impossible to sustain logistically.

Preparing Now for an Uncertain Future

CENTCOM must add to its already heavy task list the force training for CENTCOM attached units that may be employed in the CAS. These may include courses, exercises, and engagement by linguists, Special Operations Forces, National Guard units, and Air and Coast Guard forces.

Training the Force

A shortfall that should be addressed first is linguistic training, which affects our assessment of the intelligence situation and our effective engagement. CENTCOM must clearly state its increased training requirement for total force linguists by the Defense Language Institute for all CAS languages. Other significant shortfalls in training include formal UN peacekeeping education and MOUT operations. With ethnic conflict caused by spillover—the most probable future challenge for the CAS—UN involvement becomes a question of when, not if. Leadership and conduct of these unique operations will be necessary skills that CENTCOM forces must possess.

Enabling the Force: Infrastructure Design

CENTCOM must invest in increasing the MOG according to operations plan (OPLAN) development. CENTCOM's focus on a handful of airfields will enhance force protection and allow a more rapid timeline for project completion.

Transportation Infrastructure. In conjunction with USTRANSCOM, CENTCOM must constantly update all plans/suitability reports and ensure that flight/navigation standard evaluations have been concluded as soon as possible. Other methods of transport—particularly suitable land routes connecting the airfields to users—should also be investigated by USTRANSCOM to create logistically feasible OPLAN options.

Communications Infrastructure. Not only are CENTCOM's options constrained by logistics but by communications as well. Satellite coverage giving CENTCOM its reachback capability is limited. J6 contracts for extra bandwidth, specifically commercial bandwidth, should be negotiated today as first-right-of-refusal.[63] Other CENTCOM activities that would enhance information backbones in the CAS will increase military possibilities and promote faster information exchange between regional CAS structures. Culturally, increasing information exchange and access to world information systems will increase the scope and perception of CAS leaders. Integrated air defense, border security surveillance tools, and effective military logistics can even be shared among CAS partners once robust communications are in place. Public relations, psychological operations, and other information warfare options also become available to CENTCOM and CAS militaries through the proliferation of communications systems. Close coordination with the Joint Spectrum Center, Joint Command and Control Warfare Center, and US Information Agency will help CENTCOM build effective communications systems in the CAS.

Military–Civilian Airlift Contracts. With the tremendous demand for logistics being routed by air, CENTCOM (via USTRANSCOM) contracts should ensure early access to the major US freight carriers and Civil Reserve Air Fleet assets. Already running freight into all five of the CAS, DHL International, Federal Express, and United Parcel Service can actually outperform Air Mobility Command deliveries by getting freight there in two to five days.[64] Negotiations should be expanded to include assets like airlines

currently transporting CENTCOM personnel into South-
west Asia (i.e., Tower Air, American Trans Air, etc.).

Organizing the Force

According to CENTCOM personnel, the delegation of
Central Asia in CENTCOM's AOR and US European Command's area of interest only brought two billets with it. Re-
viewing each functional area needs to be accomplished to
ensure there are adequate billets. Additionally, with the
significant threat of humanitarian tragedy (e.g., ethnic
conflict), CENTCOM more than any other unified command needs to pioneer a robust civil-military operations
center (CMOC) capability. Then commander of Operation
Restore Hope, Lt Gen Anthony C. Zinni, USMC, noted that
"instead of thinking about warfighting agencies like command and control, you create a political committee, a civil
military operations center—CMOC—to interface with volunteer organizations. These become the heart of your operations, as opposed to a combat or fire support operations
center."[65] A list of organizations that are notionally engaged is available in Joint Publication 3-08, *Interagency
Coordination During Joint Operations*, volume 2, and
should serve as the basis for the CMOC.[66] This CMOC
should apply the lessons CENTCOM learned in Operation
Restore Hope by investing in the staffing and education of
permanent CMOC personnel. Just as the new concept of
the "Aerospace Operations Center as a weapons system"
will ensure properly trained full-time manning, a CENTCOM-
sponsored "CMOC as a weapons system" can be a revolu-
tionary way to get the DOD to realize the importance of the
command and control of military operations other than
war (MOOTW).

Coordinating with the Force

CENTCOM's imperative of global engagement begins
with shaping the environment. CENTCOM–State Department liaisons remain vital in the national pursuit of unity
of effort. Coordinated planning, funding, and executing
strategies must build on each other synergistically to promote stability and prevent ethnic violence in the region.
CENTCOM needs to use its liaisons to develop procedures

that allow ease of FMS/EDA and WMD clean-up challenges discussed earlier that will make military engagement more successful. These issues need four-star endorsement today in CENTCOM's quest to prepare for an uncertain tomorrow.

Commitment

"A key ingredient in successful intervention is the credibility of the international commitment. External interventions that the warring parties fear will soon fade may be worse than no intervention at all. Ambiguous policies signal weaker parties that they may do better by fighting longer and harder than compromising for what they can get now. In today's world there is no practical alternative to an international community actively engaged over the long term in containing ethnic conflict."[67] In the past, it has required "boots on the ground" to show US resolve. In terms of ethnic conflict or spillover, all that may be required is heightened military-military contact or a precisely timed air-drop exercise. But in Central Asia, where ethnic issues have been around for many years, the US effort must also last many years. Applying the military IOP must be clearly thought out, applied evenhandedly throughout the CAS, and must be sustainable. To do so will take creative planners and equally creative coalitions such as the ones built during Operation Desert Storm. Arab, European, Russian, Chinese partners, partners with other CAS, and partnerships with nongovernmental and private volunteer organizations will be the only successful strategy to deal with ethnic conflict and spillover within this volatile region.

Summary

So what is the biggest threat to CENTCOM in Central Asia? I have demonstrated that ethnic violence caused by spillover from neighboring countries will be the most likely problem. Conflict in the CAS should cause CENTCOM great concern because of the incredibly high stakes. The region's WMD, their resources, US regional influence, and the fact that this geographical crossroad has all of the most powerful countries in the world watching is the exact reason why the United States must maintain its global engagement in Central Asia focused on promoting stated US interests.

To attain those national goals, we must engage all IOPs as an integrated force. The United States can little afford to rely on sanctions like those that took seven years to work in Libya as their primary means of securing the area as a stable democratic region. The price of standing still is just too high. CENTCOM must engage now in all five of the CAS fostering a regional approach to security. This is the only way to make each of the ethnic groups feel represented and thus less threatened. But that is only one solution.

To achieve stability, promote democracy, and ensure our national security, CENTCOM must consider the nature of ethnic conflict, the principles of insurgent warfare and MOOTW, and develop a thoughtful strategy that creates a new regional vision for Central Asia. That strategy—built with the discussions of this paper—should use the following tenets as a framework:

- Does the plan rely on a regional approach? Demand integration of each country?

- Does the plan consider reactions by the Shanghai Five? Turkish and Iranian reaction?

- Is the plan sustainable with clear goals attainable in both the near and far term?

- Is there burden sharing with Asia and Europe, the prime recipients of CAS oil?

- Does the plan build on the US ability to introduce forces into the CAS if necessary?

- Does the plan add to the legitimacy of the current government?

- Does the plan assign accountability to the government for its treatment of ethnic groups?

- Is the plan fully integrated or congruent with all other IOPs and the NSS/NMS?

In responding to these questions, CENTCOM planners should be looking for positive answers that will ensure a synergistic approach.

The United States once again has the opportunity to shape the future of countries much like the Marshall Plan did. In their wildest dreams, the authors of that plan probably could not have envisioned that in 50 years the rubble of Europe would be a bustling center for one of the most powerful economic unions in the world. Hopefully, CENTCOM will have just such a vision for Central Asia.

Notes

1. Ted Robert Gurr, *Why Men Rebel* (Princeton, N.J.: Princeton University Press, 1970).

2. Timothy D. Sisk, *Power Sharing and International Mediation in Ethnic Conflicts* (New York: Carnegie Corporation, 1996), 119.

3. "History of Central Asia," n.p., on-line, Internet, 5 December 1999, available from http://members.tripod.com/~kz2000/history/centas.html.

4. Stephen and Sandra Batalden, *The Newly Independent States of Eurasia: Handbook of Former Soviet Republics* (Phoenix, Ariz.: Oryx Press, 1997), 178.

5. Mike Edwards, "A Broken Empire: Kazakhstan," *National Geographic Magazine*, March 1993, 29.

6. David Lake and Donald Rothchild, "Containing Fear: The Origins and Management of Ethnic Conflict," in *Theories of War and Peace: An International Security Reader*, Michael E. Brown, ed. (Cambridge, Mass.: MIT Press, 1998).

7. Michael Brown, "Causes and Regional Dimensions of Internal Conflict," in *The International Dimensions of Internal Conflict*, Michael Brown, ed. (Cambridge, Mass.: MIT Press, 1966), 577.

8. Ibid., 578.

9. Ibid., 574.

10. Library of Congress country studies gave great statistical data. "Table 3. Central Asia: Population Distribution 1989–1992 (in thousands)," n.p., on-line, Internet, 15 November 1999, available from http://lcweb2.loc.gov/frd/cs/uzbekistan/uz_appen.html; and "Table 4. Central Asia: Ethnic Composition, Selected Years, 1989–94 (in percentages)," n.p., on-line, Internet, 15 November 1999, available from http://lcweb2.loc.gov/frd/cs/uzbekistan/uz_appen.html.

11. Stanley Escudero and Olivier Roy, *Special Report on Tajikistan: The War in Tajikistan Three Years On* (Washington, D.C.: US Institute of Peace Press, 1996).

12. Graham Fuller, "Central Asia: The Quest for Identity," *Current History*, April 1994, 148.

13. Iran's supreme chief of state is the cleric ayatollah Khomeini, and the president is pro-western Hatami. "Iran," Central Intelligence Agency, *World Factbook*, n.p., on-line, Internet, 10 December 1999, available from http://www.odci.gov/cia/publications/factbook/geos/ir.html; *A National Security Strategy for a New Century* (Washington, D.C.: Government Printing Office [GPO], December 1999), 33; and "Iran: Reformist Majority

Undermines Theocracy," n.p., on-line, Internet, 9 February 2000, available from http://www.stratfor.com/MEAF/commentary/m000209011 5.htm.

14. "Fundamentalist Threat Rising in Central Asia," n.p., on-line, Internet, 9 February 2000, available from http://www.stratfor.com/services/giu/021898.asp.

15. William M. Tart, "Afghanistan: Same as it Ever Was." Written 20 January 2000 to fulfill partial completion of American Military University course LC508. The Jamiat-i-Islami (Society of Islam) led by Burhaniddin Rabanni and his defense minister, Ahmad Shah Massoud, are the legitimate recognized government of Afghanistan.

16. "Fundamentalist Threat Rising in Central Asia."

17. Fuller, 149.

18. Uzbekistan, Tajikistan, and Kyrgyzstan. Nancy Lubin, Keith Martin, and Barnett R. Rubin, *Calming the Ferghana Valley* (Washington, D.C.: Brookings Press, 1999).

19. Ibid.

20. Stephen Van Evera, "Hypotheses on Nationalism and War," in *Theories of War and Peace*, Michael E. Brown, ed., 266.

21. Peter Grier, "New World Coming," *Air Force Magazine*, December 1999, 59–62.

22. Ibid.

23. Brown, "Causes and Regional Dimensions of Internal Conflict," 465.

24. Van Evera, 273.

25. Samuel P. Huntington, "The Clash of Civilizations?" *Foreign Affairs*, Summer 1993, 17–19. That line, generally speaking, can be drawn east-west through Kazakhstan.

26. Van Evera, 274.

27. Amy Myers Jaffe and Robert A. Manning, "The Shocks of a World of Cheap Oil," *Foreign Affairs*, January–February 2000, 16–29.

28. *A National Security Strategy for a New Century* (Washington, D.C.: GPO, 1999), 1.

29. Ibid., 2.

30. Ibid.

31. Ibid.

32. Ibid., 3.

33. Ibid.

34. As a matter of fact, significant CTR funds have already been spent just in Uzbekistan and Kazakhstan. With the remaining former Soviet nuclear weapons in storage in Uzbekistan and the growing legacy of environmental issues surrounding Soviet WMD programs in Kazakhstan, both countries have requested increases in CTR funding for the foreseeable future. Unfortunately, some of the funding is requested for clean-up of previous WMD facilities.

35. Chief of Army General Staff Bakhytzhan Ertaev and businessman Aleksandr Petrenko went on trial and were convicted in January 2000. Ertaev implicated the former prime minister, but no charges were filed. The complete story of the transaction is on this Web site. "The High Price of Kazakhstan's MiG Affair," n.p., on-line, Internet, 5 January 2000, available from http://www.stratfor.com/services/giu/111899.asp.

36. Oil reserves: United States (22 billion barrels), North Sea (17 billion barrels); the entire Caspian Sea region estimates (16–32 billion barrels). Natural gas proven reserves: North America (300 trillion cubic feet) and Kazakhstan, Turkmenistan, Uzbekistan (236–337 trillion cubic feet). Caspian region, n.p., on-line, Internet, 5 January 2000, available from

http://www.eia.doe.org/emeu.cabs/caspian.html and "Caspian Tables, Maps," n.p., on-line, Internet, 5 January 2000, available from http://www.eia.doe.gov/emeu/cabs/caspgrph.html.

37. Uzbekistan increased its oil production by more than 91,000 barrels per day in only five years while Turkmenistan added 23,000 barrels per day to its output over an eight-year period. "Caspian Sea Region" (16–32 billion barrels) and "Turkmenistan" (236–337 trillion cubic feet), n.p., on-line, Internet, 5 January 2000, available from http://www.eia.doe.gov/emeu/cabs/turkmen.html and "Uzbekistan," n.p., on-line, Internet, 5 January 2000, available from http://www.eia.doe.gov/emeu/cabs/uzbek.html.

38. Kazakhstan has seen a slump by 30,000 barrels a day over the past seven years. "Caspian Tables, Maps" and "Kazakhstan," n.p., on-line, Internet, 5 January 2000, available from http://www.eia.doe.gov/emeu/cabs/kazakh.html.

39. 1997 CAS oil production from the Caspian was a respectable 763,000 barrels a day.

40. Turkmenistan with the world's third largest natural gas reserves behind Russia and Qatar.

41. From Chinese and American joint ventures that have developed agreements to build the world's longest pipeline, a natural gas pipeline to a Chinese coastal port to the Japanese, German, US, Korean, and Swiss refurbishment tenders on CAS refineries, there is widespread evidence of international interest.

42. Although critical to the stability of their economies, these refineries are not state of the art and have hurt overall CAS production. Kazakhstan has three refineries undergoing various stages of upgrades. They have changed hands numerous times due to improprieties and legal issues. Here, poor performance of oil and the output and transport fees by KazakhOil and KazTransOil (both former Soviet-style firms) hurt profits. Learning their lesson from this dependence, Kazakhstan is building a natural gas liquification plant in conjunction with Phillips and a new gas processing plant in order to limit Russian Gazprom influence. For its role, Turkmenistan has only two refineries; and they are engaged with the French to build a new lubricant blending facility at the port city of Turkemenbashi. Uzbekistan has two older refineries and one newer refinery that were built since the breakup. They have a brand new petrochemical plant and, innovatively, they plan to have 360 compressed natural gas filling stations by 2004 to take advantage of their immense gas resource.

43. Uzbek produced more than 1,700 metric tons in 1997. They will almost double that in 2000 with a proposed 3,000 metric tons of 38,000 tons of reserves.

44. "Central Asian Nuclear Weapons Free Zone," n.p., on-line, Internet, 12 March 2000, available from http://www.fas.org/nuke/control/canwfz.

45. *A National Security Strategy for a New Century*, 2.

46. Ibid., 33.

47. The Organization for Security and Cooperation in Europe's (OSCE) field office and base of operations in the CAS is in Kyrgyzstan. "Kyrgyzstan," *CIA World Factbook 1999*, n.p., on-line, Internet, 3 February 2000, available from http://www.odci.gov/cia/publications/factbook/kg.html.

48. George Tanham, *War without Guns: American Civilians in Rural Vietnam* (New York: Praeger, 1966), 23–30.

49. Escudero and Roy, available from http://www.usip.org/oc/sr/tajik2.html. French scholar Roy is former head of the OSCE mission to Dushanbe, Tajikistan; and Ambassador Escudero was the United States's chief representative in Dushanbe.

50. This information was extracted from media ratings from CENT-COM documents.

51. Drug trafficking route aids in transporting illegal drugs.

52. "DEA Foreign Offices," n.p., on-line, Internet, 20 December 1999, available from http://www.usdog.gov/dea/briefingbook/page8.htm. Particular problems are with Kyrgyzstan and Tajikistan.

53. Escudero and Roy.

54. Andrew Bell–Fialkoff, *Ethnic Cleansing* (New York: St. Martin's Press, 1996).

55. "Fundamentalist Threat Rising in Central Asia," n.p., on-line, Internet, 9 February 2000, available from http://www.stratfor.com/services/giu/021898.asp.

56. Chairman of the Joint Chiefs of Staff (CJCS), *National Military Strategy, Shape, Respond, Prepare Now: A Military Strategy for a New Era*, Washington, D.C., 11.

57. Max G. Manwaring, "The Manwaring Paradigm," in *Low-Intensity Conflict: Old Threats in a New World*, Edwin G. Corr and Stephen Sloan, eds. (Boulder, Colo.: Westview Press, 1992).

58. A USN commander comments during his 20 January 2000 lecture in Wood Auditorium, Air Command and Staff College, Air University, Maxwell Air Force Base, Ala.

59. Lieutenant Colonel Hayman, "CCJ4/7 Information Paper. Subject: Security Assistance Program-Uzbekistan," 15 November 1999.

60. Escudero and Roy, 3.

61. Coast Guard courses and Special Operations Forces course titles vary based on levels of experience and requirements.

62. Although there are 11 airfields more than 10,000 feet long and deemed suitable for even C-5 operations, but maximum on the ground restricts effective war-time operations at all 11. "Airfield Suitability," n.p., on-line, Internet, 17 December 1999, available from http://www.amc.af.mil/do/doa/doas.html and also per conversation 17 December 1999 with Maj Jeff Hupy.

63. First-right-of-refusal includes a contract that allows us to decline a capability before any other customer.

64. "UPS," n.p., on-line, Internet, 22 January 2000, available from http://www.ups.com and "DHL," n.p., on-line, Internet, 22 January 2000, available from http://www.dhl.com and "Federal Express," n.p., on-line, Internet, 22 January 2000, available from http://www.fedex.com.

65. CJCS, Joint Publication (JP) 3-08, *Interagency Coordination During Joint Operations*, vol. 2, 9 October 1996, III-16-19.

66. Ibid., B-A-36–38. The list in JP 3-08 could also serve as the basis for the on-site operations coordination center in UN operations.

67. Donald Rothchild and David Lake, "Preventing Ethnic Conflict," n.p., on-line, Internet, 13 October 1999, available from http://www-igcc.ucsd.edu/IGCC2/newletterprev/newletter/study.html.

Appendix A
Ethnic Disposition

Group	Kazakhstan	Kyrgyzstan	Tajikistan	Turkmenistan	Uzbekistan
Kazakh	44.3	0.9	n/a	2	4.1
Kyrgyz	n/a	52.4	n/a	n/a	0.9
Tajik	n/a	0.8	64.9	n/a	4.7
Turkmen	n/a	n/a	n/a	73.3	0.6
Uzbek	2.2	12.9	25.1	9.1	71.4
Russian	35.8	21.5	3.5	9.8	8.3
Ukranian	5.1	2.5	n/a	n/a	0.8
German	3.6	2.4	n/a	n/a	n/a
Uigher	n/a	0.9	n/a	n/a	n/a
Rural	44.1	64.9	71.9	54.9	61.3
Urban	55.9	35.1	28.1	45.1	38.7

Source: Tables 3 and 4 available from http://lcweb2.loc.gov/frd/cs/uzbekistan/uz_ appen.html.

Note: Disposition in percentage: "n/a" reflects that either they are a negligible part of the population or sources did not break them out further. Most of these groups probably were grouped into the "Other" category.

Appendix B
Defense Industries of Selected CAS

Major Defense Industry Facilities in Kazakhstan

Note: The BW/CW facility at Vozrozhdenly Island in the Aral Sea shared with Uzbekistan is depicted on the map. Sources report the north half (Kazakh) was the living quarters for Soviet scientists while the south (Uzbek) was the laboratory. (Map source available at: http://www.lib.utexas.edu/Libs/PCL/Map_collection/commonwealth/DfnsIndust-Kazakhstan.jpg; and http://www.lib.utexas.edu/Libs/PCL/Map_collection/commonwealth/DfnsIndust-Uzbekistan.jpg.

Details including satellite imagery of "Voz" Island are available at http://www.fas.org/nuke/guide/russia./facility/cbw/index.html.

Major Defense Industry Facilities in Uzbekistan

Appendix C
Central Asian Oil Infrastructure

Selected Oil Infrastructure in the Caspian Sea Region

Note: This map depicts Trans–Caspian issues. The following is a worldview that illustrates why many international powers are interested in Central Asia and its energy flow. Source available from http://www.eia.doe.gov/emeu/cabs/caspgrph.html.

Existing and Potential Oil and Gas
Export Routes from the Caspian Basin